I0415788

December 2011

TAXPAYER PRIVACY

A Guide for Screening and Assessing Proposals to Disclose Confidential Tax Information to Specific Parties for Specific Purposes

U.S. Government Accountability Office

GAO 90 YEARS 1921-2011
ACCOUNTABILITY ★ INTEGRITY ★ RELIABILITY

GAO-12-231SP

Contents

Abbreviations

FTI	federal tax information
IRC	Internal Revenue Code
IRS	Internal Revenue Service
JCT	Joint Committee on Taxation
OECD	Organisation for Economic Co-operation and Development
Treasury	Department of the Treasury

United States Government Accountability Office
Washington, DC 20548

December 14, 2011

The Honorable Max Baucus
Chairman
The Honorable Orrin G. Hatch
Ranking Member
Committee on Finance

The Honorable Charles E. Grassley
Ranking Member
Committee on the Judiciary
United States Senate

The Internal Revenue Service (IRS) receives a great deal of personal information about individuals and businesses. While taxpayers are required to provide this information to IRS under penalty of fine or imprisonment, confidentiality of information reported to IRS is widely held to be a critical element of taxpayers' willingness to provide information to IRS and comply with the tax laws. As a general rule, anything reported to IRS is held in strict confidence—Internal Revenue Code (IRC) Section 6103 provides that federal tax information is confidential and to be used to administer federal tax laws except as otherwise specifically authorized by law.

Although tax information is confidential, nondisclosure of such information is not absolute. Section 6103 contains some statutory exceptions, including instances where Congress determined that the value of using tax information for nontax purposes outweighs the general policy of confidentiality. Since making amendments to Section 6103 in 1976, Congress has expanded the statutory exceptions under which specified taxpayer information can be disclosed to specific parties for specific purposes. Today, Section 6103 exceptions enable law enforcement agencies to use relevant tax information to investigate and prosecute tax and nontax crimes and allow federal and state agencies to use it to verify eligibility for need-based programs and collect child support, among other uses.

Periodically, new exceptions to the general confidentiality rule are proposed, and some in the tax community have expressed concern that allowing more disclosures would significantly erode privacy and could compromise taxpayer compliance. In evaluating such proposals, it is important that Congress consider both the benefits expected from a disclosure of federal tax information and the expected costs, including reduced taxpayer privacy, risk of inappropriate disclosure, and negative effects on tax compliance and tax-system administration. This guide, prepared at your request, is intended to facilitate consistent assessment of proposals to grant or modify Section 6103 exceptions. This guide consists of key questions that can help in (1) screening a proposal for basic facts and (2) identifying policy factors to consider. A description of how we developed this guide begins on p. 5.

As agreed with your offices, unless you publicly announce the contents of this guide earlier, we plan no further distribution until 30 days from the report date. At that time, we will send copies to interested congressional committees, the Director of the Office of Management and Budget, Secretary of the Treasury, Commissioner of Internal Revenue, and other interested parties. In addition, the guide will be available at no charge on the GAO website at http://www.gao.gov.

If you have any questions about this guide, please contact me at (202) 512-9110 or brostekm@gao.gov. Contact points for our Offices of Congressional Relations and Public Affairs may be found on the last page of this report. Key contributors to this guide are listed in appendix IV.

Michael Brostek
Director
Strategic Issues

Laws Protecting FTI Confidentiality

Federal tax information (FTI)—tax returns and return information (as defined in fig. 1 below)—is kept confidential under Section 6103 of the IRC except as specifically authorized by law. Information in a form that cannot be associated with or otherwise identify, directly or indirectly, a particular taxpayer is not FTI. Section 6103 specifies what FTI can be disclosed, to whom, and for what purpose.[1] Prior to passage of Section 6103 amendments in the Tax Reform Act in 1976, the executive branch had discretion over decisions to share taxpayer information. The 1976 amendments were written to address concerns about the potential for too much dissemination of tax information and the misuse of tax information.[2]

Figure 1: Definitions of Tax Return and Tax-Return Information

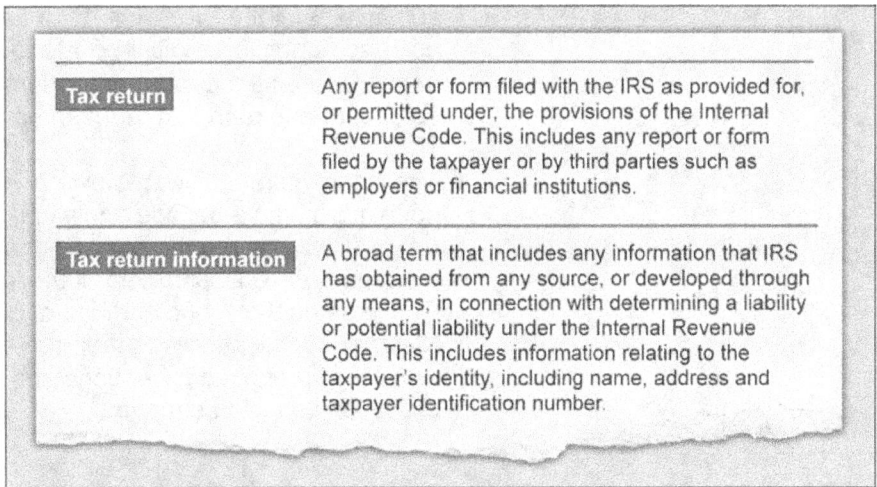

Tax return	Any report or form filed with the IRS as provided for, or permitted under, the provisions of the Internal Revenue Code. This includes any report or form filed by the taxpayer or by third parties such as employers or financial institutions.
Tax return information	A broad term that includes any information that IRS has obtained from any source, or developed through any means, in connection with determining a liability or potential liability under the Internal Revenue Code. This includes information relating to the taxpayer's identity, including name, address and taxpayer identification number.

Source: Internal Revenue Code.

In general, FTI is collected and developed to administer tax law. This information, however, can be useful for other purposes, such as to detect possible noncompliance with nontax criminal laws or administer other kinds of government programs. In 1976 and since, Congress has granted

---

[1]This report focuses on potential exceptions in Section 6103 that would enable IRS to disclose a taxpayer's information to a third party without the taxpayer's authorization. This report is not focused on disclosures made by IRS to a third party at the request or consent of the taxpayer whose information is to be disclosed.

[2]The history of Section 6103 has been discussed in many previous reports. Please see the selected bibliography at the end of this report.

some statutory exceptions to confidentiality and repealed or modified certain existing exceptions. Congress also has considered but not enacted other proposals. Congress has generally attempted to balance the expectation of taxpayer privacy with the competing policy goals of efficient use of government resources, the public health and welfare, and law enforcement. Exceptions to the general rule of confidentiality can be very narrowly prescribed. For example, for the purpose of determining creditworthiness for a federal loan, the law authorizes the IRS to disclose to a federal agency whether or not a loan applicant has a delinquent tax debt, but not more information than that.[3] The law grants more-general disclosures of FTI to state tax agencies for the administration of state taxes. Additionally, Section 6103 authorizes disclosures for nontax administration purposes to specific entities such as certain congressional committees or the President or for specific purposes such as statistical use or determining eligibility for federal programs.[4] Appendix I has more information on the current exceptions to FTI confidentiality, including safeguard and reporting requirements.

The last comprehensive reviews of the Section 6103 framework were done more than a decade ago when the IRS Reform and Restructuring Act of 1998 required the Joint Committee on Taxation (JCT) and the Secretary of the Department of the Treasury (Treasury) to report to Congress on the scope and use of Section 6103 provisions regarding taxpayer confidentiality. In their reports, JCT and Treasury called for strict scrutiny of proposed exceptions and the circumstances when such exceptions should be made. [5]

---

[3]26 U.S.C. 6103(l)(3).

[4]Properly authorized GAO employees also have access to FTI used in federal agencies' programs or activities. Such access is granted by congressional committees with jurisdiction over tax matters on a case-by-case basis. In such cases, FTI may be disclosed to only those GAO employees who have a need to examine the information in the performance of their official duties and responsibilities as necessary to audit the selected federal program or activity.

[5]Joint Committee on Taxation, *Study Of Present-Law Taxpayer Confidentiality And Disclosure Provisions As Required By Section 3802 Of The Internal Revenue Service Restructuring And Reform Act Of 1998*, vols. 1-3 (Washington, D.C.: January 2000); and Department of the Treasury, *Report to the Congress on Scope and Use of Taxpayer Confidentiality and Disclosure Provisions*, vol. 1, "Study of General Provisions" (Washington, D.C.: October 2000).

How This Guide Was Developed

To identify what criteria or other policy factors Congress might wish to consider when deciding whether to grant exceptions to the general rule of tax information confidentiality, we reviewed

- Treasury and JCT reports;
- congressional reports and hearing records dated between 1999 through April 2011 with references to Section 6103, including proposals enacted and not enacted;
- available research on the effect of tax-information confidentiality on voluntary tax compliance;[6]
- Treasury and IRS criteria used in assessing proposals to disclose tax information for nontax purposes,[7]
- the Fair Information Practices; and
- GAO internal guidance for recommendations on using tax data for nontax purposes.

The Fair Information Practices were a key basis for this guide. First proposed in 1973 by a U.S. government advisory committee, the Fair Information Practices are now widely accepted and, with some variation, the basis of privacy laws and related policies in the United States and many countries. They are also reflected in a variety of federal-agency policy statements on information privacy. The Fair Information Practices are not precise legal requirements. Rather, they provide a framework of principles for balancing the need for privacy with other public policy interests, such as national security, law enforcement, and administrative efficiency. Included in the practices is the principle that the collection and use of data should be limited to specific purposes and that individuals should have ready means of learning about the collection and use of information about them. Appendix II has more information on the Fair Information Practices.

We drafted guide questions and revised them based on feedback from Treasury, IRS, JCT, and the National Taxpayer Advocate as well as parties representing tax practitioners, privacy advocates, and private-

---

[6]Voluntary compliance refers to the reliance of the income tax system, in part, on taxpayers reporting and paying their taxes as required with no direct enforcement and minimal interaction with the government.

[7]IRS's 1994 memorandum republished in app. B of Treasury's 2000 report elaborates on these criteria.

sector business concerns.[8] We selected them to get views from parties that represent different perspectives and with expertise in tax administration, privacy, and information issues. We provided a draft of this guide to officials from Treasury and IRS for comment regarding facts and incorporated their comments as appropriate.

We conducted our work from December 2010 to December 2011 in accordance with all sections of GAO's Quality Assurance Framework that are relevant to our objectives. The framework requires that we plan and perform the engagement to obtain sufficient and appropriate evidence to meet our stated objectives and to discuss any limitations in our work. We believe that the information and data obtained, and the analysis conducted, provide a reasonable basis for any findings and conclusions.

How to Use This Guide

This guide was developed to assist and inform decision making regarding proposed statutory exceptions to tax information confidentiality or modifications to existing exceptions. It is intended to help policymakers think about important factors and competing interests rather than to provide a single right answer or optimal decision.

The guide consists of two sections of key questions for evaluating Section 6103 exception proposals, as shown in figure 2. The first section includes five threshold questions for screening proposals to address basic issues, such as whether they are adequately developed and tailored to minimize disclosure of confidential tax information. Under this framework, all of the threshold questions would be resolved with a "yes" answer before further consideration of the proposal. The second section includes six policy-factor questions that explore the proposal's expected benefits and costs,[9] privacy effect and safeguards, and effects on the tax system. Generally the policy questions deal with issues of magnitude, or "how much." These

---

[8]Parties included the American Civil Liberties Union, American Institute of Certified Public Accountants, Center for Democracy and Technology, Consumer Data Industry Association, Robert Gellman (privacy and information policy consultant), National Association of Enrolled Agents, and National Association of Tax Professionals.

[9]The Office of Management Budget (OMB) provides guidance on conducting cost-benefit economic analysis that can be used to systematically assess program or policy options to maximize benefits achieved with resources used. Although this guide uses the terms benefits and costs, these terms are used generally as broad categories of, respectively, desired and undesired effects of a given proposal, not as defined and used in cost-benefit economic analysis.

questions help identify trade-offs to consider among policy factors as well as potential risks to mitigate. In summary, the questions and their answers are intended to support a determination of whether approving the confidentiality exception is the best alternative. The order of the threshold and policy questions reflects a logical sequence of important issues that should all be given careful consideration. Appendix III is a full list of the threshold and policy-factor questions and subquestions discussed throughout the body of the guide.

Figure 2: Threshold and Policy-Factor Questions for Assessing Any Proposal to Disclose Confidential Tax Information

Directions:

Mouseover the following threshold and policy-factor questions to reveal important subcategory questions to consider.

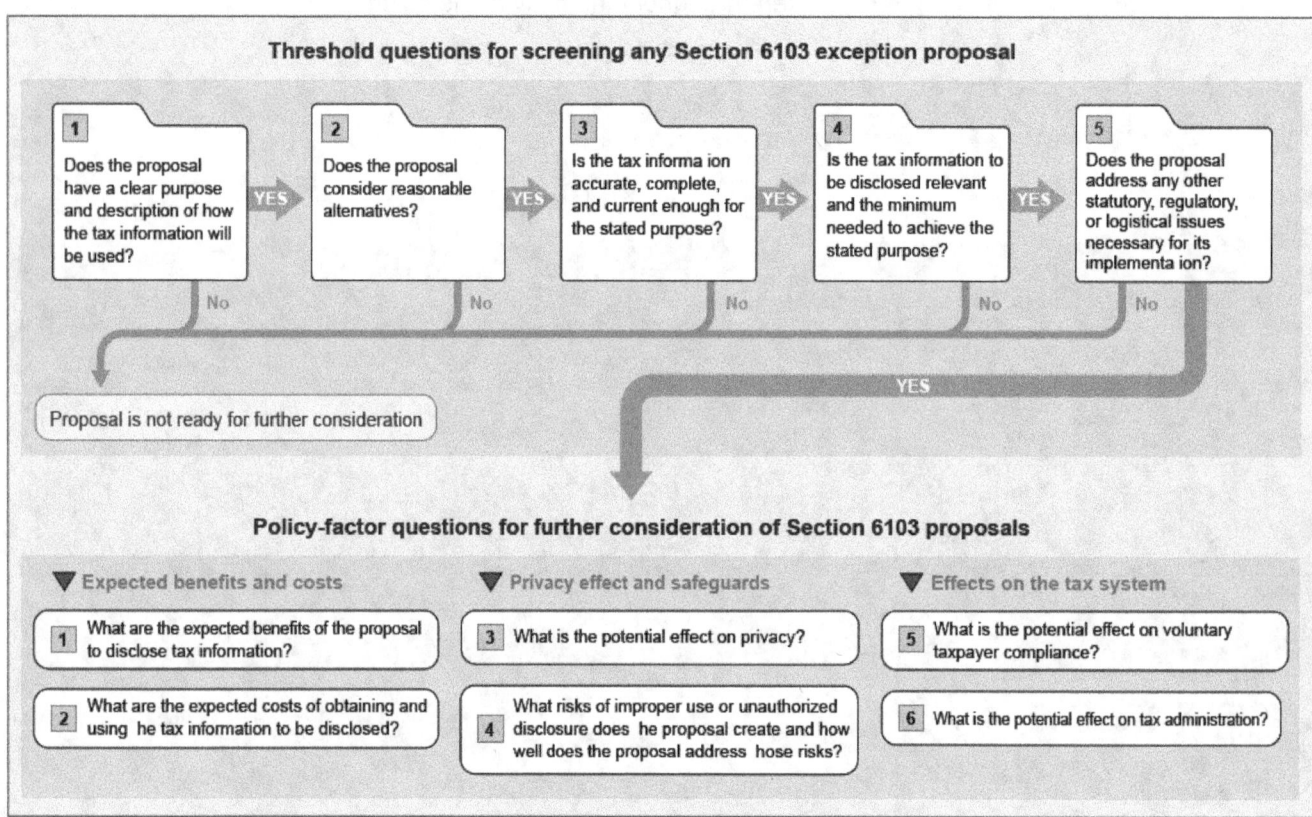

Threshold questions for screening any Section 6103 exception proposal

1	2	3	4	5
Does the proposal have a clear purpose and description of how the tax information will be used?	Does the proposal consider reasonable alternatives?	Is the tax informa ion accurate, complete, and current enough for the stated purpose?	Is the tax information to be disclosed relevant and the minimum needed to achieve the stated purpose?	Does the proposal address any other statutory, regulatory, or logistical issues necessary for its implementa ion?

YES → YES → YES → YES →

No / No / No / No / No

YES

Proposal is not ready for further consideration

Policy-factor questions for further consideration of Section 6103 proposals

▼ Expected benefits and costs

1 What are the expected benefits of the proposal to disclose tax information?

2 What are the expected costs of obtaining and using he tax information to be disclosed?

▼ Privacy effect and safeguards

3 What is the potential effect on privacy?

4 What risks of improper use or unauthorized disclosure does he proposal create and how well does the proposal address hose risks?

▼ Effects on the tax system

5 What is the potential effect on voluntary taxpayer compliance?

6 What is the potential effect on tax administration?

Source: GAO.

Print instructions | To print text version of this graphic, go to appendix III.

GAO-12-231SP Taxpayer Privacy Guide

The guide is intended both for evaluating FTI disclosure proposals having an expected tax benefit or tax-specific use as well as proposals for other types of benefits or uses not directly related to tax administration. Whether proposed uses, particularly disclosures for uses beyond tax administration, are seen as appropriate depends in part on how one views the role of tax information held by IRS. Some have advocated that FTI should be used only for tax administration and not disclosed outside of IRS. Others believe that FTI should be used as any other government information resource to achieve non-tax-related policy ends. In between these two positions is the view that FTI disclosures are acceptable in some cases but must be well justified. Regardless of one's view, the questions in this guide are designed to support evaluating the relevant important taxpayer privacy rights, tax-system effects, and other key issues raised by proposals to disclose FTI. This guide may also assist Congress with oversight of existing exceptions to confidentiality under Section 6103.

Evaluating a proposal to use tax information will likely involve considerable judgment because objective information about likely effects may not be available. Therefore when developing and assessing an FTI disclosure proposal, it would be beneficial to build in mechanisms, such as performance reporting requirements, to assess the exception after it is implemented. It would, of course, be appropriate to weigh the cost of complying with any such reporting requirements against the expected value of the reports.

Threshold Questions for Screening Section 6103 Exception Proposals

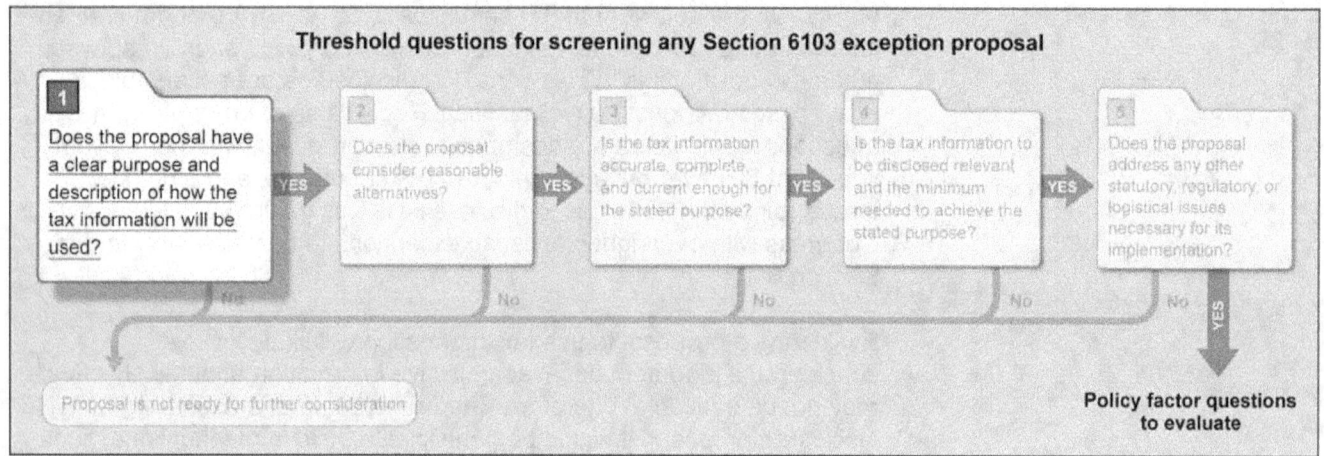

Threshold questions for screening any Section 6103 exception proposal

1. Does the proposal have a clear purpose and description of how the tax information will be used? YES→
2. Does the proposal consider reasonable alternatives? YES→
3. Is the tax information accurate, complete, and current enough for the stated purpose? YES→
4. Is the tax information to be disclosed relevant and the minimum needed to achieve the stated purpose? YES→
5. Does the proposal address any other statutory, regulatory, or logistical issues necessary for its implementation?

No → Proposal is not ready for further consideration

YES → Policy factor questions to evaluate

Source: GAO

Threshold Question 1: Does the proposal have a clear purpose and description of how the tax information will be used?

The first step in answering the threshold and policy-factor questions is to have a clear description of basic elements of the exception proposal and its intended purpose. The description should detail the following:

- What specific information will be disclosed?
- To whom will the information be disclosed?
- What category or categories of taxpayers will be affected?
- How will the information be used?
- What purpose will be achieved?

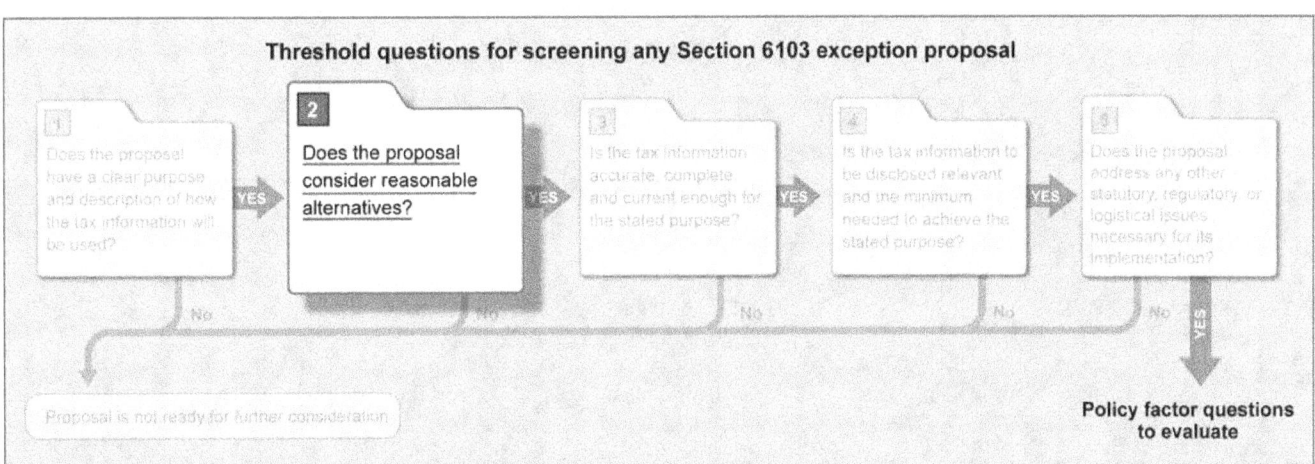

Threshold questions for screening any Section 6103 exception proposal

1	Does the proposal have a clear purpose and description of how the tax information will be used?
2	Does the proposal consider reasonable alternatives?
3	Is the tax information accurate, complete, and current enough for the stated purpose?
4	Is the tax information to be disclosed relevant and the minimum needed to achieve the stated purpose?
5	Does the proposal address any other statutory, regulatory, or logistical issues necessary for its implementation?

Proposal is not ready for further consideration

Policy factor questions to evaluate

Source: GAO

Threshold Question 2: Does the proposal consider reasonable alternatives?

Any disclosure of tax information comes with costs and creates risks. These are discussed in detail in the policy-factor questions below. In order to consider a proposal, however, it is important that such consideration be done in light of any reasonable alternatives. Assessing a proposal's alternatives could involve a separate evaluation of the alternatives using this guide, though much of this framework is specific to FTI disclosures.

One alternative for some proposals may be to obtain the information through taxpayer consent, as permitted under Section 6103(c). For example, when applying for home loans, taxpayers often consent to have income information from their tax returns disclosed to a mortgage company for verification. These disclosures are not subject to the safeguards otherwise required by Section 6103 as a condition for entities to receive tax information from IRS. However, other restrictions on the information may apply, such as the Privacy Act in the case of federal agencies receiving tax information pursuant to taxpayer consent. The Section 6103 safeguard requirements are discussed later in the safeguards policy-factor question and in appendix I.

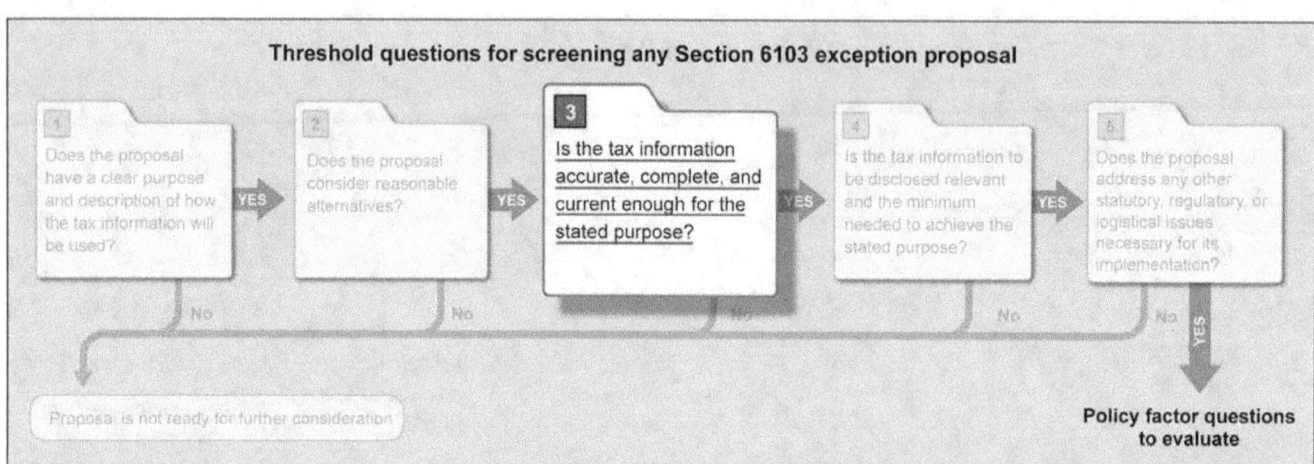

Threshold questions for screening any Section 6103 exception proposal

1. Does the proposal have a clear purpose and description of how the tax information will be used? — YES →
2. Does the proposal consider reasonable alternatives? — YES →
3. Is the tax information accurate, complete, and current enough for the stated purpose? — YES →
4. Is the tax information to be disclosed relevant and the minimum needed to achieve the stated purpose? — YES →
5. Does the proposal address any other statutory, regulatory, or logistical issues necessary for its implementation? — YES → **Policy factor questions to evaluate**

No → Proposal is not ready for further consideration

Source: GAO.

Threshold Question 3: Is the tax information accurate, complete, and current enough for the stated purpose?

Any proposal to disclose and use FTI depends on the information being accurate and complete enough to use and available when it is needed. One challenge related to disclosure proposals stems from the errors that tax information can contain. Information reported to IRS by tax filers and third parties is not always accurate. IRS may also introduce errors when processing the information, for example when transcribing tax information from paper returns. IRS finds and corrects some errors in the course of its return processing and examination processes, but not all of them.

Consideration should also be given to whether tax information is sufficiently complete for the stated purpose. Certain groups are underrepresented in IRS tax data because not everyone is required to file income-tax returns. For tax year 2010, single people under the age of 65 earning less than $9,350, and married people both under the age of 65 jointly earning less than $18,700, were not required to file tax returns. Also, some individuals and businesses that are supposed to file returns fail to do so.

Additionally, tax information should be sufficiently current for the stated purpose when first used and for any later uses. Some FTI is only available for use outside of IRS after a lag time of more than a year. Taxpayers' tax returns and information from third parties are generally provided to the IRS after a tax year, and the information provided may be as much as 17 months old. IRS processing then takes more time, including time to go back to tax filers and third parties to correct errors that IRS catches during processing. Taxpayers can also obtain deadline extensions of up to 6 months. For some proposed uses of FTI, these time lags could make FTI insufficiently current. A proposal's limits on how long information can be used—to potentially include controls such as retention limits—may address any concerns about disclosed information becoming outdated for later use.

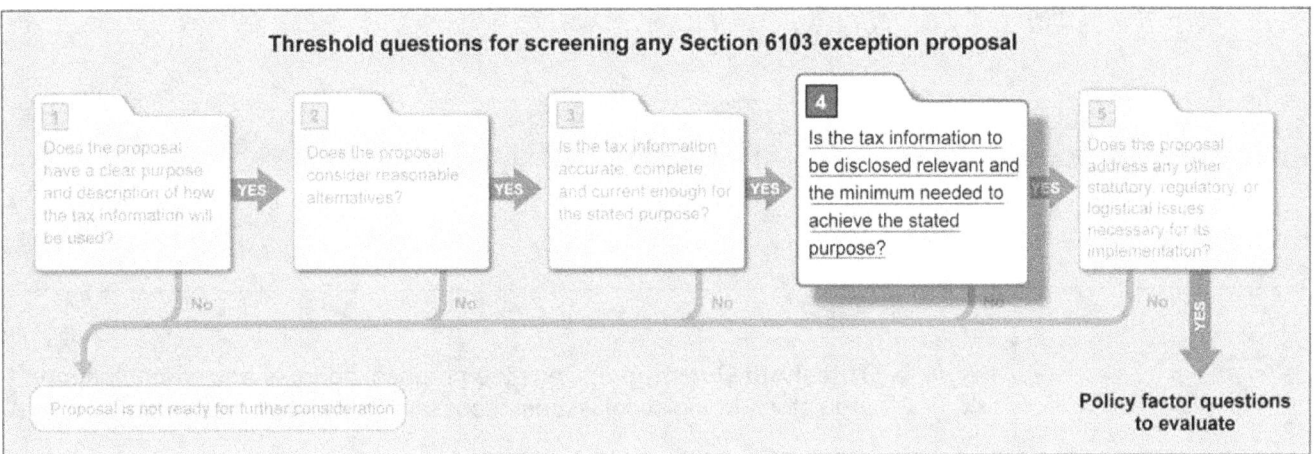

Threshold questions for screening any Section 6103 exception proposal

1. Does the proposal have a clear purpose and description of how the tax information will be used? **YES** →
2. Does the proposal consider reasonable alternatives? **YES** →
3. Is the tax information accurate, complete, and current enough for the stated purpose? **YES** →
4. Is the tax information to be disclosed relevant and the minimum needed to achieve the stated purpose? **YES** →
5. Does the proposal address any other statutory, regulatory, or logistical issues necessary for its implementation?

No → Proposal is not ready for further consideration

YES → Policy factor questions to evaluate

Source: GAO.

Threshold Question 4: Is the tax information to be disclosed relevant and the minimum needed to achieve the stated purpose?

A key consideration of any proposal is whether the information to be shared is clearly relevant to the proposed use. Only truly needed information should be disclosed, so a proposal should be tailored to ensure that each discrete element of information to be disclosed is relevant and necessary to accomplish the stated purpose. Minimizing the information disclosed to only that which is necessary can yield desirable results across several of the policy factors addressed elsewhere in this document, including reducing the costs of the disclosure (policy-factor question 2), preventing an unwarranted invasion of privacy (policy-factor question 3), or reducing the risk of unauthorized disclosure or use (policy-factor question 4). Such consideration is evident in IRS's implementation of the privacy exception that provides for public disclosure of certain information about payment agreements between IRS and persons settling a tax debt for less than the full amount. While the name of the person entering into the agreement is disclosed, the Internal Revenue Manual requires that tax identification numbers, addresses, and certain other information be redacted.

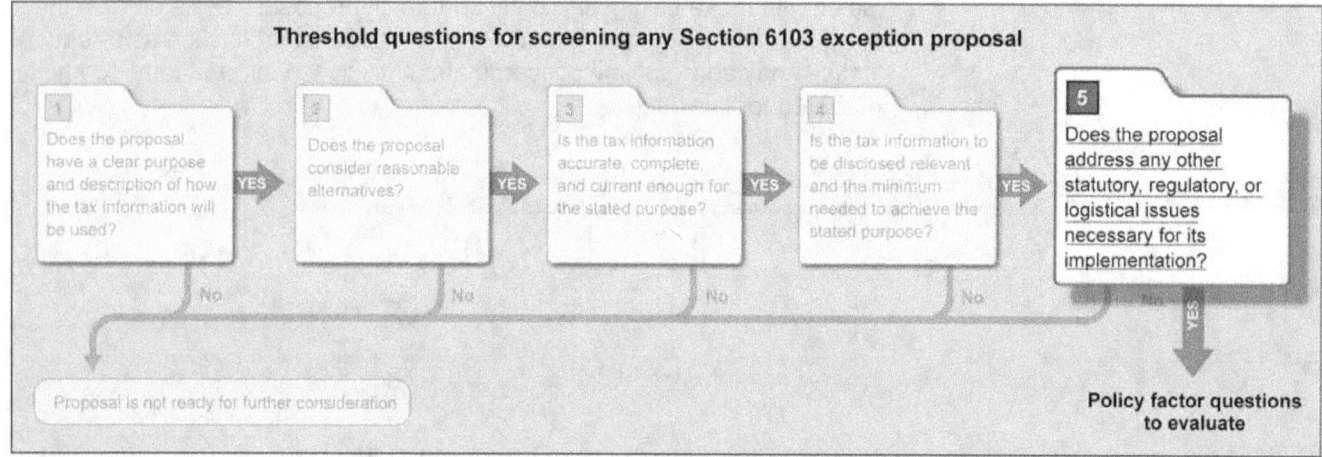

Source: GAO.

Threshold Question 5: Does the proposal address any other statutory, regulatory, or logistical issues necessary for its implementation?

- Will the proposal require additional legislation besides modifying section 6103 to accomplish the desired result?
- Does the proposal conflict with existing regulations, rules, or statutes other than Section 6103?
- How will any logistical or practical barriers or hindrances to implementing the proposed disclosure and use of information for the stated purpose be resolved?

Changes to Section 6103 protections may not be the only changes needed to implement the proposed use of FTI. Other needed changes can be legal or logistical and may cause the proposal to be unnecessarily difficult, costly, or even impossible to implement. For example, other statutes, regulations, or practices may restrict or preclude the disclosure, access, and use of FTI for the stated purpose. Furthermore, agencies may not have systems or staffing in place to make use of the information. Also, agency practices might preclude the specified use. For example, if an agency uses contractors to do program work that would require handling of the disclosed tax information, then the proposal would have to address not only disclosure to agency employees but also to contractors.

Identifying all needed statutory, work-process, and information-flow changes can help assure that all the steps necessary to implement the proposal are clearly spelled out.

Policy-Factor Questions for Further Consideration of Section 6103 Proposals

After an FTI disclosure proposal has been screened with the threshold questions (and each of the thresholds has been met), the proposal's costs and benefits can be systematically assessed using the policy-factor questions below. Although they are discussed separately, policy questions may be interrelated. For example, a proposal may mean that IRS has to devote more resources to oversee FTI safeguards, which could potentially affect other aspects of tax administration (policy-factor question 6). Also, the significance of each issue discussed below likely will vary for any given FTI disclosure proposal.

Expected Benefits and Costs

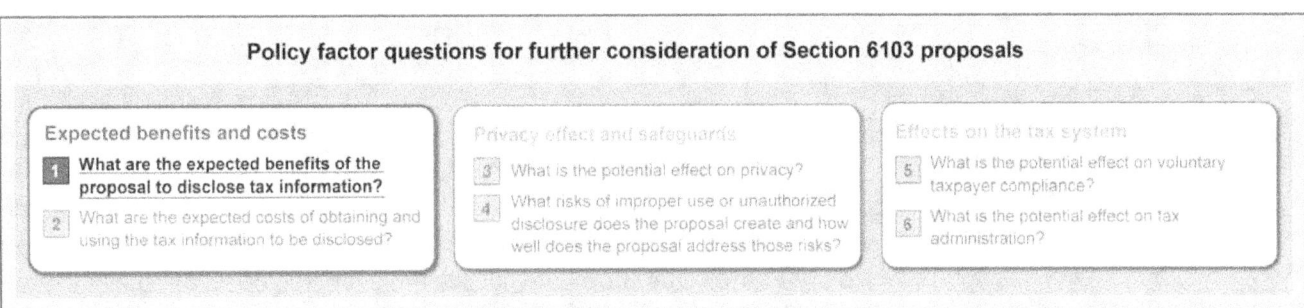

Policy factor questions for further consideration of Section 6103 proposals

Expected benefits and costs
1. What are the expected benefits of the proposal to disclose tax information?
2. What are the expected costs of obtaining and using the tax information to be disclosed?

Privacy effect and safeguards
3. What is the potential effect on privacy?
4. What risks of improper use or unauthorized disclosure does the proposal create and how well does the proposal address those risks?

Effects on the tax system
5. What is the potential effect on voluntary taxpayer compliance?
6. What is the potential effect on tax administration?

Source: GAO.

Policy-Factor Question 1: What are the expected benefits of the proposal to disclose tax information?

- What are the estimated financial benefits, if any, to be achieved by using tax data?
- What are the nonfinancial benefits that are expected, if any?

A proposal could involve anticipated financial benefits such as saving money by reducing improper payments or making better decisions about government-backed loans. A proposal could also have nonfinancial benefits, such as improving the accuracy or reliability of government statistical information. Some proposals may include a combination of financial and nonfinancial benefits. For example, a previous FTI disclosure proposal involved disclosing FTI to the Department of Education to streamline the application process for federal financial aid for postsecondary education. This proposal was intended to reduce the Department of Education's application-processing burden and improper payments related to inaccurate income reporting on the financial-aid application. The benefits were also expected to extend to families and schools that participated in the financial-aid programs by simplifying the application process.

To the extent possible, a proposal should specify and quantify its expected benefits. Benefits may include positive effects on voluntary compliance or tax administration, which are discussed specifically in questions five and six below.

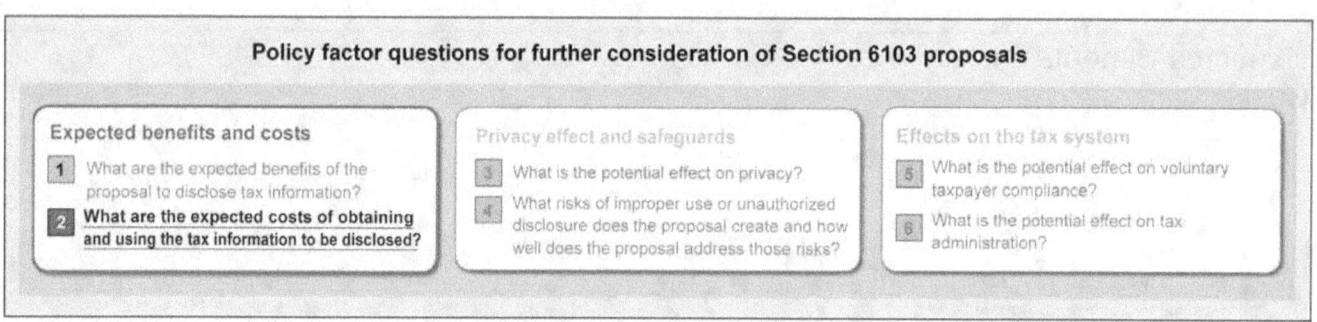

Policy factor questions for further consideration of Section 6103 proposals

Expected benefits and costs	Privacy effect and safeguards	Effects on the tax system
1 What are the expected benefits of the proposal to disclose tax information?	3 What is the potential effect on privacy?	5 What is the potential effect on voluntary taxpayer compliance?
2 What are the expected costs of obtaining and using the tax information to be disclosed?	4 What risks of improper use or unauthorized disclosure does the proposal create and how well does the proposal address those risks?	6 What is the potential effect on tax administration?

Source: GAO.

Policy-Factor Question 2: What are the expected costs of obtaining and using the tax information to be disclosed?

- What are the estimated costs for IRS to provide the tax data?
- What are the estimated costs to the entity receiving the information?
- What are the expected costs for others affected by the tax-disclosure proposal?

Policymakers need to be able to consider all of the expected financial costs associated with the proposed use of FTI. Such costs would likely include costs to IRS, such as those for compiling and transmitting the data, as well as for accounting for the disclosures and providing oversight to ensure that the recipient of the data has the necessary safeguards in place to protect taxpayer information, ensure confidentiality, and prevent misuse. Section 6103 outlines the recordkeeping, safeguarding, reporting, and IRS oversight requirements that are conditions for receiving returns and return information.[10] Costs to IRS would also depend on whether IRS's current processes and information systems are capable of providing the requested information or if changes are needed to implement the proposal. For the entity receiving the information, a key consideration is the cost of establishing and maintaining the previously mentioned safeguards—a condition for any entity to receive tax information. To the extent that any entities besides IRS and the recipient of the FTI are involved, costs to those entities should also be addressed. For example, if the proposal involves changes to third-party reporting by financial institutions, the cost of meeting the new requirements should be a part of the benefit/cost discussion. Other costs may include negative effects on voluntary compliance or tax administration, which are discussed specifically in questions five and six below.

Privacy Effect and Safeguards

The benefits of privacy may be less tangible and immediate than the benefits of disclosing information to support some other purposes such as national security or law enforcement. As a result, in some cases, privacy may be at an inherent disadvantage when decision makers weigh privacy against other interests. Therefore, focused, systematic consideration of privacy is critical in assessing a proposal to disclose tax information. Safeguarding the disclosed FTI is an important aspect of protecting privacy.

---

[10]Section 6103(p)(3), and Section 6103(p)(4). These requirements are also described in IRS Publication 1075, *Tax Information Security Guidelines For Federal, State, and Local Agencies*. Under Section 6103(p)(3)(B), IRS is required to annually report an accounting for disclosures to the JCT. Additionally, IRS is required to submit a public report on disclosure to JCT under Section 6103(p)(3)(C).

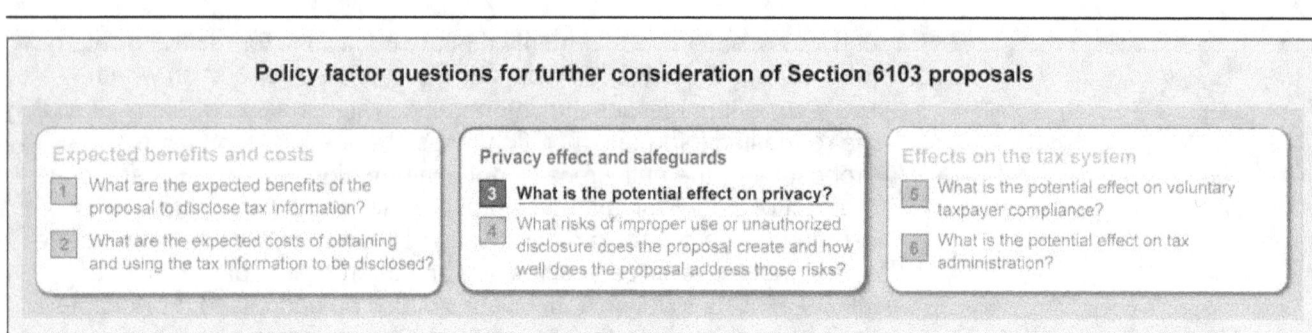

Policy factor questions for further consideration of Section 6103 proposals

Expected benefits and costs
1. What are the expected benefits of the proposal to disclose tax information?
2. What are the expected costs of obtaining and using the tax information to be disclosed?

Privacy effect and safeguards
3. **What is the potential effect on privacy?**
4. What risks of improper use or unauthorized disclosure does the proposal create and how well does the proposal address those risks?

Effects on the tax system
5. What is the potential effect on voluntary taxpayer compliance?
6. What is the potential effect on tax administration?

Source: GAO.

Policy-Factor Question 3: What is the potential effect on privacy?

- To what extent will the proposal adversely affect taxpayer privacy?
- Is the use of the information transparent and limited?
- Will sufficient notice and control be provided to individuals?

A key consideration for any FTI disclosure proposal is how much it will adversely affect privacy. Decision makers should know how many taxpayers will be involved, how much and what type of information will be disclosed, how sensitive the information is, who outside of IRS is going see that information, and the extent to which the disclosure and use of the information may adversely affect people's privacy or other interests. Making a determination about the extent of an adverse impact involves assessing how well a proposal conforms to the Fair Information Practices. As addressed in threshold questions 1 and 4, such an assessment is needed to ensure that the proposal

- has a clearly specified purpose,
- minimizes the amount of information to be disclosed, and
- limits use of the disclosed information to the specified purpose.

The Fair Information Practices state that the public should be informed about privacy policies and practices and that individuals should have a ready means of learning about the use of their personal information. This is particularly important when the government is involved. The Fair Information Practices say it is important to ensure that information collected for one government function is not used indiscriminately for other, unrelated functions. Furthermore, the practices say that collection of personal information should be performed, where appropriate, with the knowledge or consent of the individual. Additionally, the practices say that it is important that there be transparency about how information is protected and that limits are placed on what information the government maintains.

Because tax information is generally recognized as being collected and developed to administer tax laws, its use for other purposes needs to be transparent. It should be clear what the government is doing with FTI and what limits will be placed on how the receiving entity may use the information. It is also important that taxpayers receive notice about the use of their information. Therefore, decision makers should determine if the proposal does these things adequately. On the basis of the practices, specific questions to consider, where appropriate, include the following:

- Will taxpayers be given sufficient, timely notice of the FTI disclosure and use?
- Will taxpayers be given the opportunity to disallow the disclosure?
- Will sufficient procedures be in place to give taxpayers access to the disclosed information, opportunities to correct any inaccurate information, and notification of access and correction procedures?
- Will sufficient notice be given to affected taxpayers regarding privacy policies and practices, such as the safeguards that will be in place for disclosed information, including security, retention, and disposal?

As noted earlier, the practices are not precise legal requirements; rather, they provide a framework of principles for balancing the need for privacy with other public-policy interests. Therefore the above questions—such as whether to provide taxpayers notice of, and opportunity to disallow, a disclosure—will not necessarily lead to such procedures in all cases. The privacy benefits of giving taxpayers prior notice or control over the disclosures would need to be justified in light of possible program risks or costs of such procedures. For example, it may not be appropriate to inform taxpayers that FTI about them is being used in a criminal investigation. It also may not be useful to report all disclosures to federal agencies for statistical or audit and evaluation purposes.

Means already exist to implement Fair Information Practices for uses of FTI. For example, the Section 6103 legal framework itself—by which only Congress can authorize use of tax information for other purposes—is part of the controls to prevent indiscriminate use of FTI for other purposes. Moreover, openness about how FTI is used and protected is addressed through publicly available information about Section 6103 and FTI safeguards, including the content of the law itself. In addition, publications specifically about IRS privacy practices and the safeguards afforded FTI are available from IRS.[11] IRS also provides general notices about how the information provided by taxpayers can be used. For example, in the instructions for the widely used Form 1040, IRS refers to its authority to disclose tax returns and return information to others and provides several examples of such uses.

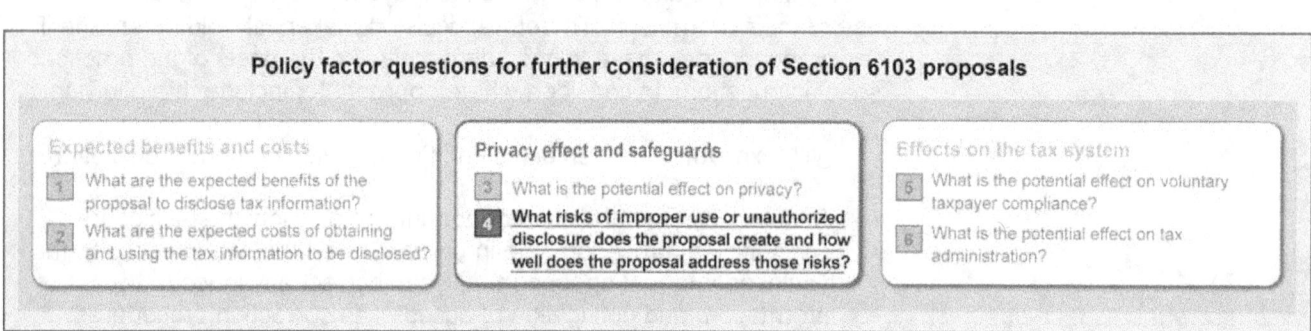

Policy factor questions for further consideration of Section 6103 proposals

Expected benefits and costs	Privacy effect and safeguards	Effects on the tax system
1 What are the expected benefits of the proposal to disclose tax information?	3 What is the potential effect on privacy?	5 What is the potential effect on voluntary taxpayer compliance?
2 What are the expected costs of obtaining and using the tax information to be disclosed?	4 **What risks of improper use or unauthorized disclosure does the proposal create and how well does the proposal address those risks?**	6 What is the potential effect on tax administration?

Source: GAO.

Policy-Factor Question 4: What risks of improper use or unauthorized disclosure does the proposal create and how well does the proposal address those risks?

- Does the proposal adequately take into account risks of unauthorized use or redisclosure associated with the disclosure?
- Does the proposal provide adequate safeguards to mitigate those risks?

Fair Information Practices call for reasonable security safeguards against risks such as loss or unauthorized access, destruction, use, modification, or disclosure. According to the internal control standards for the federal government, no matter how well designed and operated, no system of controls can provide absolute assurance that an objective will be met—in this case, that information is perfectly safe from improper use or unauthorized disclosure—so assessment and mitigation of risk is critical

---

[11]For example, Internal Revenue Service, *Tax Information Security Guidelines For Federal, State and Local Agencies*, Publication 1075 (Washington, D.C.: August 2010); and *Disclosure and Privacy Law Reference Guide*, Publication 4639 (Washington, D.C.: September 2011).

to providing reasonable assurance that the disclosed FTI will be protected.[12] Another important risk consideration involves data mining or other techniques that may allow someone to merge different sets of seemingly anonymous, aggregated data to identify specific individuals. Policymakers should consider how well the proposed use of FTI addresses the risks of improper use or unauthorized disclosure that could be created if the proposal is adopted.

Section 6103 and IRS Publication 1075 specify the safeguard requirements that entities receiving tax information must have in place to prevent the information from being misused, that is, used for an unauthorized purpose, or disclosed without authorization.[13] Agencies that receive FTI are required to maintain a permanent system of standardized records on the use and disclosure of the information, store the information in a secure area, restrict access to the tax information, and properly dispose of the information after use. To further reduce the risk of misuse or unauthorized disclosure, a proposal may require that the tax information be returned to IRS or destroyed after it is no longer useful or after a set period. Safeguards are subject to periodic IRS review.

Effects on the Tax System

The expected benefits and costs associated with an FTI disclosure proposal were discussed previously under the policy-factor questions concerning expected benefits and costs. The potential effects on voluntary compliance and tax administration, discussed here, may represent either benefits or costs. Because continued willingness of taxpayers to provide their personal information is critical to voluntary compliance and tax administration, any proposed disclosure's effect on such willingness warrants specific consideration.

---

[12]GAO, *Standards for Internal Control in the Federal Government*, GAO/AIMD-00-21.3.1 (Washington, D.C.: November 1999).

[13]Section 6103(p)(4). Criminal and civil sanctions that apply to the unauthorized disclosure and inspection of tax information are under separate sections of the Internal Revenue Code (IRC §§ 7213 and IRC §§ 7431, respectively); and are generally described in Internal Revenue Service Publication 1075. Additional requirements include those of the Federal Information Security Management Act of 2002.

Policy factor questions for further consideration of Section 6103 proposals

Expected benefits and costs

1 What are the expected benefits of the proposal to disclose tax information?

2 What are the expected costs of obtaining and using the tax information to be disclosed?

Privacy effect and safeguards

3 What is the potential effect on privacy?

4 What risks of improper use or unauthorized disclosure does the proposal create and how well does the proposal address those risks?

Effects on the tax system

5 **What is the potential effect on voluntary taxpayer compliance?**

5 What is the potential effect on tax administration?

Source: GAO.

Policy-Factor Question 5: What is the potential effect on voluntary taxpayer compliance?

- What is the potential effect on voluntary compliance by taxpayers whose tax information will be disclosed?
- What is the potential effect on general voluntary compliance for other taxpayers?

Tax information is collected and developed for the primary purpose of tax administration. Some in the tax community are concerned that granting exceptions to confidentiality could compromise voluntary taxpayer compliance. Voluntary compliance happens when a taxpayer files tax form(s) on time that accurately report tax liability and, if applicable, pays on time the amount of tax due as required by the Internal Revenue Code. Disclosures of tax information can have a range of voluntary compliance effects, either positive or negative (as a benefit or a cost, respectively), so a proposal should be subject to a systematic consideration of possible voluntary compliance effects. Some proposals may enhance voluntary compliance. For example, if participation in a federal program is contingent on past compliance with the tax laws, people may be encouraged to stay compliant. Negative compliance effects are also possible. For example, people may think twice about filing a tax return or properly reporting all of their income if they know that the information may be used by an agency besides IRS in a way that they believe will disadvantage them.

The positive or negative effects on voluntary compliance may be limited to the individuals whose tax information is disclosed by IRS, or it may have broader effects on taxpayers in general. One possible general effect of increased use of FTI by entities other than IRS could be a sense among taxpayers that the information reported to IRS is not kept private, so providing information to IRS is a bad idea. For example, according to IRS research, nonfiling of tax returns increased after Treasury began to offset tax refunds to collect nontax debts owed to the government.[14] On the other hand, when IRS contacts third parties for information regarding suspected hidden income or assets, it necessarily discloses that there is some sort of tax law enforcement action in process. When taxpayers are aware that such disclosures may occur, they may be more likely to comply with the tax laws because they feel they have a greater chance of being caught if they do not comply.

Limited research is available on the relationship between tax-information confidentiality and voluntary tax compliance. Voluntary compliance is complex and it may not be possible to pinpoint the effects of existing disclosures or future effects of proposed new ones. Moreover, each proposal is likely to have unique potential effects on voluntary compliance. Therefore, a proposal should include a careful assessment of potential effects on voluntary compliance for the directly affected taxpayers and taxpayers in general. Such information could include, for example

- the number of taxpayers affected,
- the number and types of tax returns that might not be filed or might be filed inaccurately and resulting types and amounts of information that might not be reported or be reported inaccurately, and
- the revenue effect of such noncompliance.

Because of uncertainty about a given proposal's effect, such quantitative data could be estimated as a range of potential effects.

---

[14]As reported in Department of the Treasury, *Report to the Congress on Scope and Use of Taxpayer Confidentiality and Disclosure Provisions.* Tax-refund offsets involve disclosure of FTI because the entity receiving the offset funds sees information about the taxpayer whose refund was offset, namely that the taxpayer was owed a refund.

Policy factor questions for further consideration of Section 6103 proposals

Expected benefits and costs	Privacy effect and safeguards	Effects on the tax system
1 What are the expected benefits of the proposal to disclose tax information?	**3** What is the potential effect on privacy?	**5** What is the potential effect on voluntary taxpayer compliance?
2 What are the expected costs of obtaining and using the tax information to be disclosed?	**4** What risks of improper use or unauthorized disclosure does the proposal create and how well does the proposal address those risks?	**6** **What is the potential effect on tax administration?**

Source: GAO.

Policy-Factor Question 6: What is the potential effect on tax administration?

- How much will implementing the proposal affect current IRS activities or performance?
- How much will any related safeguard responsibilities add to IRS's current responsibilities?

As with effects on voluntary compliance, disclosures of tax information can negatively or positively affect tax administration. In most cases, it is likely that a proposal to provide information will place more responsibilities on IRS or otherwise increase the agency's workload. Even if IRS has the data on hand and transmitting them would be simple, IRS will incur some cost to provide the information. Costs will be greater in the likely event that IRS will have to take special steps to extract the information and establish detailed transmittal protocols. If IRS needs to verify the information or correct errors before transmitting it, then the burden on IRS will be even greater. In addition, IRS will likely be responsible for ensuring that the receiving entity has adequate safeguards in place (as discussed in policy-factor question 4), and this will also require IRS staff time and other resources. All of these potential uses of IRS resources will mean either additional funding needs for IRS or the diversion of resources from other functions, perhaps resulting in adverse effects in other areas.

Effects on IRS's operations are not necessarily negative. The expected benefits of some proposals may include improved service or enforcement on the part of IRS. For example, one existing disclosure exception authorizes IRS to publish in newspapers the names of taxpayers who are owed refunds but that IRS cannot locate. In this case, the disclosure may help IRS fulfill a part of its mission and save money because the agency does not have to take more-costly steps to locate these taxpayers.

Appendix I: Internal Revenue Code Section 6103—Current Taxpayer Confidentiality and Disclosure Provisions, and Safeguard and Record-Keeping Requirements

Current Taxpayer Confidentiality and Disclosure Provisions

Under Internal Revenue Code (IRC) § 6103, tax returns and tax-return information are confidential and may not to be disclosed unless specifically authorized. However, Congress has enacted some exceptions to confidentiality. Table 1, below, provides a high-level description of current exceptions and where they are found in IRC § 6103.[1]

Table 1: Summary of IRC Section 6103 Exceptions to the General Rule of Tax-Return and Return-Information Confidentiality

IRC subsection	Description
6103(c)	Disclosure to taxpayer's designees with taxpayer's consent; provides access for anyone the taxpayer designates, although the Internal Revenue Service (IRS) has the authority to withhold the information if it determines that such disclosure would seriously impair federal tax administration.
6103(d)	Disclosure to states and regional income-tax agencies for the purpose of administration of tax laws and for carrying out combined federal and state employment-tax-reporting programs.
6103(e)	Provides for individuals' access to their own tax information and access for persons with material interest, for example, a spouse, a partner in a partnership, the administrator or executor of an estate, or an attorney authorized by the taxpayer.
6103(f)	Disclosure to committees of Congress and their agents; includes GAO.
6103(g)	Disclosure to the President and designated employees of the Office of the President, upon written request signed by the President personally. The request shall include the specific reason why the inspection or disclosure is requested, and the President shall file a report with the Joint Committee on Taxation (JCT) quarterly disclosing such requests. Authorized representatives of the President or head of any federal agency may request a tax-compliance check for prospective appointees.
6103(h)	Disclosure for the purpose of tax administration to certain federal officers and employees, including the Departments of the Treasury and Justice.
6103(i)	Disclosure to federal employees for administration of nontax laws, including access to returns and return information for use in federal criminal investigations by order from a federal judge; return information from a source other than the taxpayer or taxpayer's representative can be disclosed without a judicial order; allowing for disclosure to apprise appropriate officials of criminal or terrorist activities or emergency circumstances; and disclosure to locate fugitives from justice.

---

[1] The disclosure of certain returns and return information of tax-exempt organizations, trusts claiming charitable deductions, and certain pension plans are under IRC § 6104. The disclosure of certain written determinations and related background information are under IRC § 6110. However, information identifying the taxpayer is redacted from the document before it is released pursuant to Section 6110. Some subsections include authorization for the Social Security Administration to disclose tax-related information, for example wage information from employers contained in W-2 Wage and Income Statement forms.

IRC subsection	Description
6103(j)	Disclosure for statistical use by the Bureau of Census and the Bureau of Economic Analysis of the Department of Commerce; Bureau of Economics of the Federal Trade Commission to administer economic surveys of corporations; Department of the Treasury for preparing economic or financial forecasts, projects, analyses, and statistical studies and related activities; Department of Agriculture for the Census of Agriculture; and the Congressional Budget Office for the long-term models of the Social Security and Medicare programs. Under this provision, returns and return information are not disclosed in a form that can be associated with or identify a particular taxpayer.
6103(k)	Disclosure for certain miscellaneous tax-administration purposes, including disclosure of accepted offers-in-compromise; disclosure to foreign governments under an income-tax convention or bilateral agreement; disclosure to state agencies regulating tax preparers; and disclosure to the Financial Management Service for levies on certain government payments.
6103(l)	Disclosure for purposes other than tax administration, including disclosure to the Social Security Administration, disclosure that an applicant for a federal loan has a delinquent tax account; disclosure to federal, state, and local child-support agencies, and disclosure for the administration of the Medicare and Medicaid programs.
6103(m)	Disclosure of taxpayer-identity information to the media to notify persons entitled to a tax refund when the Secretary of the Treasury has been otherwise unable to locate the taxpayer.
	Disclosure of the mailing address of a taxpayer to certain federal agencies when necessary, including a federal agency trying to collect or compromise on a federal claim against the taxpayer; the National Institute for Occupational Safety and Health for locating individuals who are or may have been exposed to occupational health hazards; and the Department of Education or Department of Health and Human Services for locating a taxpayer who has defaulted on student loans.
6103(n)	Disclosure to contractors maintaining systems for processing and storing tax information for tax-administration purposes.
6103(o)	Disclosure with respect to taxes on tobacco, firearms, and explosives to officers and employees of the agency whose official duties require such inspection or disclosure; and disclosure with respect to taxes on wagering.

Source: GAO.

Of the 7 billion disclosures reported in the annual public-disclosure report for calendar year 2010, 99 percent were disclosed under three provisions—about 60 percent (over 4 billion disclosures) were made to state government officials for tax-administration purposes; about 21 percent (nearly 1.5 billion disclosures) were made to congressional committees and their agents, including disclosures to GAO; and about 18 percent (almost 1.3 billion disclosures) were made to the Bureau of the Census. According to the Internal Revenue Service (IRS), some disclosure provisions are rarely or never exercised.

Safeguard Requirements

To safeguard taxpayer privacy and ensure confidentially, Section 6103 imposes the following requirements for government entities receiving returns and return information from IRS:[2]

- establish and maintain a permanent system of standardized records of requests including the reason for such requests, date of requests, and any disclosures;
- establish and maintain a secure area for storage;
- restrict access to the information to only those whose duties or responsibilities require access and those to whom disclosures are permitted under section 6103;
- establish and maintain any other safeguards IRS deems necessary or appropriate;
- provide IRS a report describing the safeguard procedures; and
- dispose of the information in an appropriate manner after use.

Some disclosure provisions are exempted from the safeguard requirements including disclosures to the taxpayer of his or her tax information, to persons with a material interest, and to third parties for whom the taxpayer has consented to the disclosure. Also exempted are public disclosures (for example, agreements between IRS and persons settling a tax debt for less than the full amount) and disclosures limited to the taxpayer's mailing address.

Record-Keeping Requirements

IRC 6103 also requires record keeping for accountability and oversight. IRS is required to keep records of disclosures made under certain provisions and account for their volumes in a required annual report to the Joint Committee on Taxation (JCT), which in turn issues an annual report for public inspection.[3] Disclosures exempted from record-keeping requirements include certain public disclosures, disclosures to the Department of the Treasury and Department of Justice for tax-administration or litigation purposes, disclosures to persons with a material interest (for example, partners and trustees), disclosure to third parties through taxpayer consent, and disclosures to determine the eligibility for and amount of benefits for certain government programs.

---

[2]IRC § 6103(p)(4).

[3]IRC § 6103(p)(3).

Appendix II: The Fair Information Practices

In response to growing concern about the harmful consequences that computerized data systems could have on the privacy of personal information, the Secretary of Health, Education & Welfare commissioned an advisory committee in 1972 to examine the extent to to which limitations should be placed on the application of computer technology to record keeping about people. The committee's final report proposed a set of principles for protecting the privacy and security of personal information, known as the Fair Information Practices.[1] These practices were intended to address what the committee termed a poor level of protection afforded to privacy under existing law, and they underlie the major provisions of the Privacy Act, which was enacted the following year. A revised version of the Fair Information Practices, developed by the Organisation for Economic Co-operation and Development (OECD) in 1980, has been widely adopted and was endorsed by the U.S. Department of Commerce in 1981.[2] This version of the principles was reaffirmed by OECD ministers in a 1998 declaration and further endorsed in a 2006 OECD report.[3] The OECD version of the principles is shown in table 2 below.

---

[1] Department of Health, Education & Welfare, *Records, Computers, and the Rights of Citizens: Report of the Secretary's Advisory Committee on Automated Personal Data Systems* (Washington, D.C.: 1973).

[2] OECD, *Guidelines on the Protection of Privacy and Transborder Flow of Personal Data* (Sept. 23, 1980). The OECD plays a prominent role in fostering good governance in the public service and in corporate activity among its 34 member countries. It produces internationally agreed-upon instruments, decisions, and recommendations to promote rules in areas where multilateral agreement is necessary for individual countries to make progress in the global economy.

[3] OECD, *Making Privacy Notices Simple: An OECD Report and Recommendations* (July 24, 2006).

Table 2: The Fair Information Practices

Principle	Description
Collection limitation	The collection of personal information should be 1. limited, 2. should be obtained by lawful and fair means, and, 3. where appropriate, with the knowledge or consent of the individual.
Data quality	Personal information should be 1. relevant to the purpose for which it is collected, and should be 2. accurate, 3. complete, and 4. current as needed for that purpose.
Purpose specification	The purposes for the collection of personal information should be 1. disclosed before collection and upon any change to that purpose, and 2. its use should be limited to those purposes and compatible purposes.
Use limitation	Personal information should not be disclosed or otherwise used for other than a specified purpose without consent of the individual or legal authority.
Security safeguards	Personal information should be protected with reasonable security safeguards against risks such as loss or unauthorized access, destruction, use, modification, or disclosure.
Openness	1. The public should be informed about privacy policies and practices, and 2. individuals should have ready means of learning about the use of personal information.
Individual participation	Individuals should have the following rights: 1. to know about the collection of personal information, 2. to access that information, 3. to request correction, and 4. to challenge the denial of those rights.
Accountability	Individuals controlling the collection or use of personal information should be accountable for taking steps to ensure the implementation of these principles.

Source: Organisation for Economic Co-operation and Development.

Appendix III: Compilation of Guide Questions

The following threshold and policy-factor questions and subquestions are in figure 2 and throughout the body of the guide.

THRESHOLD QUESTIONS FOR SCREENING ANY SECTION 6103 EXCEPTION PROPOSAL

1. Does the proposal have a clear purpose and description of how the tax information will be used?
    - What specific information will be disclosed?
    - To whom will the information be disclosed?
    - What category or categories of taxpayers will be affected?
    - How will the information be used?
    - What purpose will be achieved?

2. Does the proposal consider reasonable alternatives?

3. Is the tax information accurate, complete, and current enough for the stated purpose?

4. Is the tax information to be disclosed relevant and the minimum needed to achieve the stated purpose?

5. Does the proposal address any other statutory, regulatory, or logistical issues necessary for its implementation?
    - Will the proposal require additional legislation besides modifying section 6103 to accomplish the desired result?
    - Does the proposal conflict with existing regulations, rules, or statutes other than Section 6103?
    - How will any logistical or practical barriers or hindrances to implementing the proposed disclosure and use of information for the stated purpose be resolved?

POLICY-FACTOR QUESTIONS FOR FURTHER CONSIDERATION OF SECTION 6103 PROPOSALS

Expected Benefits and Costs

1. What are the expected benefits of the proposal to disclose tax information?
    - What are the estimated financial benefits, if any, to be achieved by using tax data?
    - What are the nonfinancial benefits that are expected, if any?

2. What are the expected costs of obtaining and using the tax information to be disclosed?
   - What are the estimated costs for IRS to provide the tax data?
   - What are the estimated costs to the entity receiving the information?
   - What are the expected costs for others affected by the tax-disclosure proposal?

Privacy effect and safeguards

3. What is the potential effect on privacy?
   - To what extent will the proposal adversely affect taxpayer privacy?
   - Is the use of the information transparent and limited?
   - Will sufficient notice and control be provided to individuals?

4. What risks of improper use or unauthorized disclosure does the proposal create and how well does the proposal address those risks?
   - Does the proposal adequately take into account risks of unauthorized use or redisclosure associated with the disclosure?
   - Does the proposal provide adequate safeguards to mitigate those risks?

Effects on the tax system

5. What is the potential effect on voluntary taxpayer compliance?
   - What is the potential effect on voluntary compliance by taxpayers whose tax information will be disclosed?
   - What is the potential effect on general voluntary compliance for other taxpayers?

6. What is the potential effect on tax administration?
   - How much will implementing the proposal affect current IRS activities or performance?
   - How much will any related safeguard responsibilities add to IRS's current responsibilities?

Appendix IV: GAO Contact and Staff Acknowledgments

GAO Contact	Michael Brostek, (202) 512-9110, brostekm@gao.gov
Staff Acknowledgments	In addition to the contact named above, David Lewis, Assistant Director; MaryLynn Sergent, Assistant Director; John de Ferrari, Assistant Director; Marisol Cruz; Ronald Fecso, Chief Statistician; Bertha Dong; Ronald W. Jones; Shirley Jones, Assistant General Counsel; Veronica Mayhand; Donna Miller; Ellen Rominger; Cynthia Saunders; Sabrina Streagle; and Gregory Wilshusen, Director; made key contributions to this guide.

Glossary

Confidentiality	Preserving authorized restrictions on information access and disclosure, including means for protecting personally identifiable information.
Disclosure	Making a return or return information known to any person in any manner.
Fair Information Practices	A set of internationally recognized practices for addressing the privacy of information about individuals, which are the underlying policy for many national laws on privacy and data protection including the U.S. Privacy Act of 1974.
Improper payments	Any payment that should not have been made or was made in an incorrect amount under statutory, contractual, administrative, or other legally applicable requirements.
Privacy Act	The 1974 act that regulates the collection, use, dissemination, and maintenance of personal information by federal agencies. The act applies only to records about individuals that are maintained in a "system of records."
Record	Under the Privacy Act, any item or collection of information about an individual that an agency maintains and that contains that individual's name, identifying number, symbol, or other identifying particular, such as a fingerprint, voice print, or photograph.
Return	A tax or information return, declaration of estimated tax, or claim for refunds under the Internal Revenue Code, which is filed with the IRS by or on behalf of a person. Returns also include any amendments or supplements to a filed return.
Return information	Return information is broadly defined in the Internal Revenue Code to include • a taxpayer's identity, the nature, source, or amount of income, payments, receipts, deductions, exemptions, credits, assets, liabilities, net worth, lax liability, tax withheld, deficiencies, overassessments, or tax payments;

- whether the taxpayer's return was, is being, or will be examined or subject to other investigation or processing;
- any other data, received by, recorded by, prepared by, furnished to, or collected by the IRS with respect to a return or with respect to the determination of the existence, or possible existence, of liability (or the amount thereof) of any person for any tax, penalty, interest, fine, forfeiture, or other imposition or offense;
- any part of any written determination or any background file document relating to such written determination ... that is not open to inspection under section 6110 for public inspection of written determinations;
- any advance pricing agreement between the taxpayer and IRS on the taxpayer's international transactions, and related background information, entered into by a taxpayer; and
- any agreement between the taxpayer and IRS related to the taxpayer's tax liability that conclusively closes the case, and any similar agreement along with any related background information.

System of records	Under the Privacy Act, a group of records under the control of an agency from which information is retrieved by an individual's name or some other identifier assigned to that individual. The Privacy Act only applies to records about individuals maintained in a system of records.
Safeguards	Protective procedures required, as a condition for receiving tax information, for keeping the information confidential, including establishing and maintaining a permanent standardized system of records; storing the information in a secure area; restricting access to the information; returning or disposing of the information after usage is completed; providing other procedures IRS determines necessary or appropriate; and providing a report describing the established safeguard procedures to IRS upon request.
Taxpayer consent	Under Section 6103, disclosure of returns and return information to any person or persons designated by the taxpayer, subject to requirements and conditions of Department of the Treasury regulations.
Voluntary compliance	A system that relies in part on taxpayers reporting and paying their taxes as required with no direct enforcement and minimal interaction with the government.

Bibliography

This bibliography contains selected items on Internal Revenue Code Section 6103 and tax-information confidentiality.

Department of the Treasury. *National Taxpayer Advocate: 2003 Annual Report to Congress.* Washington, D.C.: December 2003.

Department of the Treasury. *Report to The Congress on Scope and Use of Taxpayer Confidentiality and Disclosure Provisions*, vol. I, "Study of General Provisions." Washington, D.C.: October 2, 2000.

Internal Revenue Service. *Tax Information Security Guidelines For Federal, State and Local Agencies*, Publication 1075. Washington, D.C.: August 2010.

Internal Revenue Service. *Disclosure and Privacy Law Reference Guide*, Publication 4639. Washington, D.C.: September 2011.

Joint Committee on Taxation. *Study of Present-Law Taxpayer Confidentiality and Disclosure Provisions as Required by Section 3802 of the Internal Revenue Service Restructuring and Reform Act of 1998*, vol. 1, "Study of General Disclosure Provisions," JCS-1-00. Washington, D.C.: January 28, 2000.

GAO's Mission	The Government Accountability Office, the audit, evaluation, and investigative arm of Congress, exists to support Congress in meeting its constitutional responsibilities and to help improve the performance and accountability of the federal government for the American people. GAO examines the use of public funds; evaluates federal programs and policies; and provides analyses, recommendations, and other assistance to help Congress make informed oversight, policy, and funding decisions. GAO's commitment to good government is reflected in its core values of accountability, integrity, and reliability.
Obtaining Copies of GAO Reports and Testimony	The fastest and easiest way to obtain copies of GAO documents at no cost is through GAO's website (www.gao.gov). Each weekday afternoon, GAO posts on its website newly released reports, testimony, and correspondence. To have GAO e-mail you a list of newly posted products, go to www.gao.gov and select "E-mail Updates."
Order by Phone	The price of each GAO publication reflects GAO's actual cost of production and distribution and depends on the number of pages in the publication and whether the publication is printed in color or black and white. Pricing and ordering information is posted on GAO's website, http://www.gao.gov/ordering.htm. Place orders by calling (202) 512-6000, toll free (866) 801-7077, or TDD (202) 512-2537. Orders may be paid for using American Express, Discover Card, MasterCard, Visa, check, or money order. Call for additional information.
Connect with GAO	Connect with GAO on Facebook, Flickr, Twitter, and YouTube. Subscribe to our RSS Feeds or E-mail Updates. Listen to our Podcasts. Visit GAO on the web at www.gao.gov.
To Report Fraud, Waste, and Abuse in Federal Programs	Contact: Website: www.gao.gov/fraudnet/fraudnet.htm E-mail: fraudnet@gao.gov Automated answering system: (800) 424-5454 or (202) 512-7470
Congressional Relations	Ralph Dawn, Managing Director, dawnr@gao.gov, (202) 512-4400 U.S. Government Accountability Office, 441 G Street NW, Room 7125 Washington, DC 20548
Public Affairs	Chuck Young, Managing Director, youngc1@gao.gov, (202) 512-4800 U.S. Government Accountability Office, 441 G Street NW, Room 7149 Washington, DC 20548